Fun with Handwriting

Name

Address

design and hand lettering by Maureen Hallahan
illustrated by Ken Chatterton

Ladybird Books

Printed letters

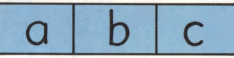

Use this page to check that you can write all the letters and numbers correctly and neatly.

Aabcdefg

The fattest part of the letter sits in the middle. Some letters have tall strokes (ascenders) and some have strokes below the line (descenders).

abcdefghijklmnopqr

stuvwxyz

123456789

ABCDEFGHIJKLMN

OPQRSTUVWXYZ

Letter families

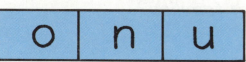

Some groups of letters start in the same place and use similar shapes. Practise these letters, then use them to make words.

o c o a g d e
   c o a g d e ➤
   dad   cog   edge   cage

n r n m h p b
   r n m h p b ➤
   none home badge bed

u u y j
   u y j ➤
   jump   judge young day
   jump   judge

Letter families

| l | v | s |

Can you think of more words using these letter families?

l
l i k f t
l i k f t ▶
life   lift   kite   bike

v
v w x z
v w x z ▶
wizard   zoo   box   voice

s
s
s ▶
spots   vase   silk   seal

Step 1

mmmmmmmmmmm

Each of these patterns is used to make and to join up different groups of letters.

mmmmmmmmmmmmmmm

mmmmmmmmmmmmmmm

r n m h

Step 2

uuuuuuuuuu

uuuuuuuuuuuuuuu

uuuuuuuuuuuuuuu

u y j i

Step 3

cccccccccc

cccccccccccccccccccccccc

cccccccccccccccccccccccc

c e a

Copy the writing patterns lots and lots of times on separate sheets of paper.

Step 4

oooooooooo

oooooooooooooooooooo

oooooooooooooooooooo

o

Step 5

More patterns for joining different letters.

mmmmmmmmmmm

mmmmmmmmmmmmm
mmmmmmmmmmmmm

m r n p q j

Step 6

ululululululul

ululululululululul
ululululululululul

ik uh li uk ah

Tail joins

uuuuuuuu

Letters join on to each other in different ways.
Tail joins are for the letters:

a c d e h i k l m n u t

am   an   in   nu

ea   ed   et   te

he   de   ie   er   der   ei

ur   en   ee   he   ut   un

Don't forget TAIL JOINS!

Horizontal joins   These are for the letters:

ooooooooooo   o r v w f

we wi vo or ro row
we wi vo or ro row

va ow run win ur re
va ow run win ur re

fi for fu

fee fi fo fum

row, row, row the boat

The f should join to the next letter by its ARM.

Diagonal joins

These are for the letters:

ch ub el il th

ch	th	eh	ub	eb	el
ch	th	eh	ub	eb	el

ok	ck	il	chl	thi
ok	ck	il	chl	thi

Practise f and l.

fl flower

fly a kite

catch the train

Break letters

s x p

Some letters don't join.

s x p g j y b

| sh | sea | ix | bo | go |
| sh | sea | ix | bo | go |

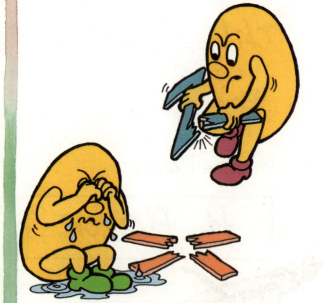

| | yo | ju | bi |
| | yo | ju | bi |

| | pi | pigs | pa |
| | pi | pigs | pa |

sheep and pigs and goats
sheep and pigs and goats

Capital letters

| A | B | C |

Most capital letters don't join on but in joined-up writing they slope forward more.

A B C D E F G H I J K L M N O P Q R

S T U V W X Y Z

C F H R

Cat Fox Horse Rabbit

Numerals

Numerals don't join on to each other or to other letters.

1 one   2 two   3 three   4 four   5 five

6 six   7 seven   8 eight   9 nine   10 ten

Let's practise

some words

Use the letters, patterns and joins that you've learned and practise writing some words you may need every day.

Sunday		
	January	July
Monday		
	February	August
Tuesday		
	March	September
Wednesday		
	April	October
Thursday		
	May	November
Friday		
	June	December
Saturday		

Let's practise

a poem

Copy the poem below.

I wish I were a little grub

With hairs around my tummy.

I'd jump into a honey pot

And make my tummy gummy.

Now write your own poem HERE!

Reasons for writing
an invitation

Look at this party invitation.
Make up your own invitation below.

Dear Jane and Tom
Please come to my party
on Saturday June 4th
at 3 Mill Street
With love from Susan

Dear..
Please come to my party
on..
at...
With love from.........................

Let's write a letter

We write to many different people. Copy this letter to Father Christmas or make up your own.

10 The Avenue
Anytown
Homeshire AB1 3LY

Dear Father Christmas,
Please send me a new book and also something nice for Mum and Dad.
With love from
Anthony

Father Christmas
Lapland
North Pole

Don't forget the address at the top.

Let's write
a shopping list

We often make a list before going shopping.

apples
soup
carrots
potatoes
milk
butter
chocolate

milk
bread

Let's write
about you

My Description

Name Steven

I am eight years of age

My height is 1.5 metres

Colour of my hair black

School St. Fred's

Draw a picture of yourself.

My name is _____

I am _____ years

My height is _____

Colour of my hair _____

Hobbies _____

Favourite Colour _____

Name of School _____

Teacher _____

Let's write the answers

Read the information and answer the questions.

Dinosaurs, whose name means 'terrible lizards', were reptiles who lived on earth millions of years ago. One of the largest dinosaurs was **Diplodocus**, shown below. It was about 27 m long, about the same as eight cars lined up nose to tail. It didn't like fighting and spent its time near water, munching plants. Because Diplodocus's teeth were not very strong it had a special stomach which helped to grind its food.

1 What does the name dinosaur mean?

2 How big was Diplodocus?

3 What was special about its stomach?

4 What did Diplodocus eat?

Let's write a signature

When you write your name on something this is called a signature.

Which of the signatures goes with each of the people at the bottom of the page?

Picasso

Wm Shakspeare

Guido Fawkes

Now practise writing your own signature.